THE LUNENBURG FARMERS' MARKET COOKBOOK

Homegrown Recipes for Every Month of the Year

RECIPES BY

Elisabeth Bailey

PHOTOGRAPHY AND FOOD STYLING BY

Alyssa Valletta

NIMBUS
PUBLISHING
— NIMBUS.CA —

Nimbus Publishing Limited
3660 Strawberry Hill Street, Halifax, NS, B3K 5A9
(902) 455-4286 nimbus.ca

Printed and bound in China
NB1689
Editor: Claire Bennet
Design: Jenn Embree
The photo on page 1 was provided courtesy of Whitney Cruikshank.

Nimbus Publishing is based in Kjipuktuk, Mi'kma'ki, the traditional territory of the Mi'kmaq People.

Library and Archives Canada Cataloguing in Publication
Title: The Lunenburg Farmers' Market cookbook : homegrown recipes for every month of the year / recipes by Elisabeth Bailey ; photography and food styling by Alyssa Valletta.
Names: Bailey, Elisabeth, author. | Valletta, Alyssa, photographer.
Description: Includes index.
Identifiers: Canadiana (print) 20230590748 | Canadiana (ebook) 20230590756 | ISBN 9781774712634 (softcover) | ISBN 9781774712825 (EPUB)
Subjects: LCSH: Seasonal cooking—Nova Scotia. | LCSH: Farmers' markets—Nova Scotia—Lunenburg. | LCSH: Cooking (Natural foods)—Nova Scotia. | LCSH: Local foods—Nova Scotia. | LCSH: Cooking—Nova Scotia. | LCSH: Cooking, Canadian—Maritime Provinces style. | LCGFT: Cookbooks.
Classification: LCC TX715.6 .B279 2024 | DDC 641.59716—dc23

Nimbus Publishing acknowledges the financial support for its publishing activities from the Government of Canada, the Canada Council for the Arts, and from the Province of Nova Scotia. We are pleased to work in partnership with the Province of Nova Scotia to develop and promote our creative industries for the benefit of all Nova Scotians.

To Naomi, the best farmers' market companion there could ever be
and
to the Mi'kmaq people, the people of this land.
We are all Treaty people.

CONTENTS

INTRODUCTION

As you might expect, dear reader, I love the many ways that local food is unique: land-based and individual to the microclimate in which it grows. The produce I buy from my friends and neighbours at the Lunenburg Farmers' Market (LFM) is not like the produce anywhere else in the world—grown in this soil, by these people, it carries the faint yet indelible stamp of home.

The other thing I love about local food, however, is the many ways in which it is absolutely *not* unique. My friends in Florida, Ontario, British Columbia, Mexico, England—they're all buying and cooking carrots and tomatoes and garlic and spinach, just like I am. And while their produce ties them to their climate and community, we can all make the same recipes and share our love for food and the importance of supporting our local food producers.

In my conversations with farmers, cooks, artisans, and other folks at the market, two themes consistently come up: creativity and community. My hope is that you find these qualities through food. Get creative with these recipes, and don't be afraid to experiment with substitutions. Talk to your farmers and ask what they like to do in their own kitchens with the products they sell. Have a question? Want to share a particularly spectacular success (or failure)?

Feel free to contact me at elisabeth.benson.bailey@gmail.com.

We're all living locally and globally at the same time. No matter where you live, this book is for you. If the LFM isn't your market, I hope you use this book as inspiration to visit one close to you and get to know the vendors selling there. And if the LFM is your market, well...see you there!

HISTORY OF
THE LUNENBURG
FARMERS' MARKET

In 1984 the idea of the Lunenburg Farmers' Market was born. Between the organizers of the then-new Bridgewater Farmers' Market and a number of Lunenburg residents—who saw the need for local food access in town—a group of eight or nine vendors came together on Thursday mornings at the old train station at the bottom of Dufferin Street, where the jitney to Mahone Bay used to drop off newspapers from Halifax before picking up salt cod at the docks.

For the majority of its early life, the market stayed small and seasonal, opening in mid-July and closing after Thanksgiving. It moved from the train station to the parking lot of the Dolphin Tavern (which later became the Lunenburg Arms) to the

Lunenburg Day Care Centre. From its first days, the market was characterized by the loyalty of its customers. Wanda Wolter of Rumtopf Farm (see page 83) says, "I remember markets where you were holding on [to] the umbrella for dear life, the rain pelting down, but the customers showed up come hell or high water."

In 2008, Lunenburg's Laughing Whale Coffee (see page 14) initiated a tiny but wonderful winter market in their café space on the corner of Lincoln and King. "We just pushed all the café tables back and made it work," Deborah d'Entremont recalls. With fresh baked goods, a fish vendor, a few artisans, and produce from both Lunenburg County and the Annapolis Valley, the winter market met a strong desire for local food in town. By the second winter it was bursting at the seams. A few years later the Lunenburg Farmers' Market took it on with Laughing Whale's blessing and became a year-round market.

As the market grew, it moved to the community centre parking lot in the summer and then inside the centre in the winter. Eventually the parking lot was needed for, well, parking, as more and more customers from across the South Shore and an increasing number of tourists came to visit. Finally, the market moved permanently indoors—using the large community centre in winter and the even larger ice rink on the other side of the parking lot in summer.

Today the market is one of the largest in Nova Scotia and is a bustling hub of activity every month of the year. Primarily a produce market, it also offers a wide variety of meat and seafood, baked goods, other edibles, and art to suit every visitor.

Visit lunenburgfarmersmarketns.ca to learn more about the LFM, and go to farmersmarketsnovascotia.ca to learn more about farmers' markets all across the province and how you can support them.

JANUARY

APPLE ACORN BREAKFAST MUFFINS

Makes 12 muffins

These muffins are the perfect grab-and-go option for a weekday morning. Bake them the evening before a busy day to power everyone through to the next sit-down meal.

INGREDIENTS

1 cup oat flour (or quick oats pulsed a few times in a blender)

1 cup whole wheat flour

2 teaspoons baking powder

1/4 teaspoon salt

2 teaspoons ground cinnamon

2/3 cup unsweetened applesauce (homemade or premade)

3/4 cup puréed cooked acorn squash

1/3 cup (or to taste) maple syrup or honey

3 tablespoons melted butter

2 eggs, room temperature

2 teaspoons vanilla extract

1 cup chopped Cortland apples (2–3 apples)

2/3 cup hickory nut or hazelnut pieces

» Preheat oven to 375°F (190°C). Generously butter a muffin tin and set aside.

» Combine oat flour, whole wheat flour, baking powder, salt, and cinnamon in a mixing bowl and whisk until thoroughly combined.

» In a second mixing bowl, combine applesauce, squash, maple syrup or honey, butter, eggs, and vanilla extract. Whisk well.

» Add dry ingredients to wet ingredients and stir until just combined.

» Add apple and hickory nut or hazelnut pieces and stir to distribute evenly.

» Transfer batter to prepared tin, filling each cup about 2/3 full. Bake until a knife inserted in the centre of one muffin comes out cleanly, about 25 minutes. After removing from oven, allow muffins to rest in the tin for 5 minutes, then transfer to a rack to cool completely.

LUNENBURG MARKET CHOWDER

SERVES 6

This recipe is flexible. Substitute other seafood or add your favourite vegetables to suit your tastes. I also like it with sweet potatoes, but any potato will work. Yukon Gold potatoes are good if you like firmer pieces, while russets will dissolve around the edges and thicken the broth a bit.

» Combine onions, butter, and salt in a stockpot over medium heat and sauté until onions are soft and fragrant, about 5 minutes.

» Add flour and whisk to combine.

» Add broth, wine, paprika, and potatoes to the pot and cover. Cook until potatoes are tender, about 15 minutes.

» Add haddock or cod and scallops. Simmer, uncovered, until just cooked through, about 5 minutes.

» Add lobster meat and coffee cream and stir until heated through, about 2 minutes.

» Remove from heat, add salt, pepper, and minced parsley (if using), and serve.

INGREDIENTS

2 onions, diced

1/4 cup butter

1/2 teaspoon salt

3 tablespoons all-purpose flour

1 1/2 cups fish or vegetable broth

2/3 cup white wine

1 teaspoon paprika

2 potatoes, peeled and cut into bite-sized pieces

1 pound (454 grams) haddock or cod fillets, cut into bite-sized pieces

1 pound (454 grams) scallops, cut into bite-sized pieces

meat from 1 cooked lobster

3 cups coffee cream

salt and pepper to taste

1/4 cup fresh minced parsley (optional)

CREAMED SPINACH

Serves 4

This is a luxurious way to enjoy spinach that pairs well with any protein-based main dish. I particularly like it with the Haddock with Browned Butter Wine Sauce on page 40.

INGREDIENTS

3 tablespoons butter

1 small onion, minced

1 generous pinch salt

1 tablespoon all-purpose flour

1 pound (454 grams, or about 10 cups) winter spinach

1 cup coffee cream

pepper to taste

» Melt butter in a large saucepan over medium heat.

» Add onion and salt and cook until softened, about 6 minutes.

» Add flour and stir well.

» Add spinach and sauté until spinach wilts completely, just a few minutes.

» Reduce heat to low and add the cream. Blend with an immersion blender.

» Add pepper and stir, continuing to cook on low until creamed spinach is thoroughly hot. Remove from heat and serve.

SAVOURY WINTER BREAD PUDDING

SERVES 6

This main dish bread pudding is a terrific use of any slightly stale bread. While it's delicious with any white loaf, the hearty flavours of the other ingredients stand up well to whole wheat or rye bread as well.

» Generously butter a casserole dish and set aside. Preheat oven to 325°F (165°C).

» Combine butter, onion, garlic, mushrooms, thyme, and rosemary in a sauté pan over medium heat. Cook, stirring often, until onion and mushrooms are cooked through and mixture is fragrant, about 5 minutes.

» Add salt and pepper to taste.

» Combine all ingredients in a mixing bowl and toss well. Transfer to the prepared casserole dish. Bake until lightly browned and cooked through, about 1 hour. Serve hot.

INGREDIENTS

2 tablespoons butter, plus extra for casserole dish

1 large onion, diced

2 cloves garlic, minced or pressed

1 cup diced mushrooms

2 teaspoons dried thyme

2 teaspoons dried minced rosemary

salt and pepper to taste

1 pound (454 grams) sausage, any kind, cooked and crumbled

1/4 cup chicken broth

2 cups grated cheese (cheddar or any other hard cheese or a combination, to taste)

8 cups cubed stale bread

5 eggs, beaten

3 cups coffee cream

CARROT CARDAMOM COFFEE CAKE

SERVES 8

Cardamom is my favourite winter spice. In this not-too-sweet treat, it pairs with cinnamon to warm your soul.

» Preheat oven to 325°F (165°C). Generously butter a large baking pan (9 x 12 or similar) and set aside.

» Combine white sugar, brown sugar, and eggs in a bowl. Beat until fluffy. Add vanilla, butter, and sour cream and beat until well combined.

» In a second bowl, combine flour, baking powder, cardamom, cinnamon, and salt. Whisk well. Add shredded carrots and toss to coat.

» Add dry ingredients to wet ingredients and mix until just combined.

» Transfer batter to prepared pan. Bake until golden and a toothpick comes out clean, about 50 minutes. Allow to cool, then serve.

INGREDIENTS

3/4 cup white sugar

3/4 cup brown sugar

4 eggs

2 teaspoons vanilla extract

1 cup butter, room temperature, plus extra for baking pan

1/2 cup sour cream

3 cups all-purpose flour

1 tablespoon baking powder

1 1/2 teaspoons ground cardamom

1 teaspoon ground cinnamon

1/2 teaspoon salt

4 cups shredded carrots

LAUGHING WHALE COFFEE ROASTERS

"**I** spend so much time chatting with customers I'm really a liability," jokes Deborah d'Entremont of Laughing Whale Coffee. She and her husband, Steve Zubalik, moved to Lunenburg in 2002 and opened up Laughing Whale the following year, bringing their coffees to market soon after. "We were so happy to be a part of it," Deborah says.

The driving force behind the Lunenburg winter market that led to the LFM becoming a year-round institution, Laughing Whale is a centre of activity at the market today. Offering a selection of fresh-brewed coffees to go as well as beans, Laughing Whale is set up and in operation in time for all the vendors to get their own coffees before the first wave of customers. It's an excellent opportunity to try a roast and then have beans ground to your specification before leaving the market.

Their coffees and other products are also available at their coffee bar on King Street.

If you think you smell coffee in the air in downtown Lunenburg, your mind isn't playing tricks on you—their low-emissions roasting facility is right next door.

In recent years Deborah and Steve have joined a coffee co-operative of twenty-five organic, fair trade roasters across Canada and the United States. The co-op builds long-term relationships with small coffee growers, such as a Muslim women's co-op in Sumatra, Indonesia. Deborah and Steve spend a few extra cents per pound to help guarantee fair wages and practices that are healthy and sustainable for both the growers and the land they grow on. "We've had some dark times in this world…. For Steve and I, it really makes it all worthwhile to feel like you're doing some good."

FEBRUARY

CLOUD EGGS

SERVES 2

Brighten up the dreariest month with this posh presentation of a breakfast classic! Add even more interest to this recipe by using a flavoured salt (such as one from OK Sea Salt, page 41).

INGREDIENTS

4 large eggs, whites and yolks separated

salt and pepper to taste

1/2 cup grated cheese, any hard kind

1/2 cup finely diced ham

smoked paprika to taste

a pinch of finishing salt

» Preheat oven to 450°F (230°C). Line a baking sheet with parchment paper and set aside.

» Combine egg whites, salt, and pepper in a large mixing bowl. Beat to stiff peaks.

» Add cheese and ham and gently fold to combine.

» Divide egg white mixture into four mounds on the prepared baking sheet. Using the back of a large spoon, create an indentation in the top of each mound.

» Bake until mounds just start to brown, about 3 minutes.

» Carefully slip an egg yolk into each indentation, sprinkle with paprika and finishing salt, and return to oven. Bake until yolks set, about 3 minutes. Serve hot.

ALL ABOUT EGGS

I love farm fresh eggs! Compared to eggs at the store, I find their shells to be harder, their yolks firmer, and even their whites less liquid. If you're new to eggs from the market, you'll find they're harder to scramble than store-bought eggs.

Like all fresh food at the market, egg availability is seasonal. Sometimes there's plenty, sometimes only a few lucky early customers snap them up. If you have more eggs than you can use within a week or two, you can always freeze them to save for leaner times.

To freeze eggs, I recommend beating them as if you were going to make scrambled eggs and adding a pinch of salt per egg (or 3/4 teaspoon for a dozen eggs). Freeze in a freezer container with a tight lid.

One final market tip: bring clean, empty egg cartons to the market for extra karma points! You can return them to the vendor who sold you the eggs or simply give them to the market manager. Farmers will reuse them for the next clutch of eggs.

FRIED GOAT CHEESE

An excellent use of the many fine flavours of goat cheese at the market, you can serve fried goat cheese plain, as a burger or sandwich topping, in a salad, or with a sauce. Marinara sauce goes well with most savoury flavours and warm honey matches well with sweet ones.

» Combine bread crumbs with salt and pepper. Toss well and set aside.

» Whisk egg and water together in a bowl and set aside.

» Form goat cheese into small balls or disks by hand, as desired.

» Place the flour on a plate. Create an assembly line with the flour, the egg wash mixture, and the seasoned bread crumbs. Take each ball or disk of goat cheese and coat with flour, then dunk in the egg wash, then coat with bread crumbs.

» Heat olive oil or butter in a sauté pan over medium heat. Fry goat cheese, turning often, until evenly golden brown, about 8–10 minutes. Serve immediately.

INGREDIENTS

1/2 cup panko (or similar) bread crumbs

salt and pepper to taste

1 egg

1 tablespoon water

2/3 cup (about 170 grams) goat cheese, chilled, any flavour

1/3 cup all-purpose flour

2 tablespoons extra-virgin olive oil (for a savoury dish) or butter (for a sweet one)

CREAMY BEET SOUP

Serves 4

Beets are more versatile than people give them credit for—this preparation showcases their inherent sweetness in a mild yet flavourful winter dish. The colour is perfect for Valentine's Day!

INGREDIENTS

3 tablespoons butter

1 pound (454 grams) beets (about 4–6 medium beets), peeled and chopped

1 large onion, diced

1 teaspoon dried thyme

4 cups chicken or vegetable broth

1 tablespoon lemon juice

3/4 cup heavy cream

salt and pepper to taste

» Melt butter in a large pot over medium heat, then add beets, onion, and thyme. Sauté until onion is softened but not browned.

» Add broth and lemon juice and increase heat to medium-high. Bring to a simmer and cook until vegetables are softened, about 20 minutes.

» Purée soup with a handheld blender, or remove to a stand blender, pureé, and return to pot. Add cream, salt, and pepper and stir well.

» Serve hot with an additional swirl of cream in each bowl, if desired.

SESAME SOY SCALLOPS

SERVES 4

I like to serve this dish in a nest of rice surrounded by julienned mixed vegetables. Feel free to adjust the crushed red pepper flakes to suit your palate.

» Combine soy sauce, garlic, vinegar, sugar, sesame oil, cornstarch, and red pepper flakes. Whisk briskly. Set aside.

» Heat large skillet over medium-high heat. Add butter, quickly swirl to coat bottom of pan, then add scallops. Cook until browned, about 2 minutes each side, flipping halfway through.

» Reduce heat to medium and add soy sauce mixture. Cook, stirring constantly, until sauce begins to thicken, 2–4 minutes.

» Remove from heat, add sesame seeds, and toss to coat. Serve.

INGREDIENTS

1/4 cup soy sauce

3 cloves garlic, minced or pressed

1 tablespoon rice wine vinegar

1 tablespoon sugar

1 tablespoon sesame oil

1 teaspoon cornstarch

1/2 teaspoon crushed red pepper flakes

2 tablespoons butter

1 1/2 pounds (680 grams) large scallops

1 heaping tablespoon sesame seeds

PEAR EAU DE VIE BREAD PUDDING

SERVES 6

This rich, sweet, eggy bread pudding is our go-to dish when we have guests for brunch. You can substitute a nut liqueur for the Pear Eau de Vie if desired, or add a complementary flavour extract instead.

INGREDIENTS

butter for casserole dish

1 loaf brioche, cut into bite-sized cubes

6 eggs

2 1/2 cups coffee cream

1/2 cup maple syrup

2 teaspoons vanilla extract

1/4 cup Ironworks Pear Eau de Vie (optional)

» Preheat oven to 350°F (177°C).

» Generously butter a large casserole dish, place bread cubes in it, and set aside.

» Combine eggs, coffee cream, maple syrup, vanilla extract, and Pear Eau de Vie (if using) in a mixing bowl and whisk together until frothy. Pour mixture over bread cubes and let stand until well soaked, about 15 minutes.

» Bake until pudding is set in centre, about 30 minutes. Serve warm or cold.

MARCH

BREAKFAST QUESADILLA

SERVES 2

Chop up your veggies the night before for quick assembly on a weekday morning.

INGREDIENTS

1/4 cup butter, divided

1 cup chopped mushrooms

1 teaspoon salt, divided

1 small onion, minced

2 cups packed chopped kale

2 eggs

2 tortillas

1 cup shredded cheese
(mozzarella, Mexican
blend, or similar)

salsa to taste

» Add half of the butter to a pan on medium-high heat, coating the bottom. Add mushrooms and half of the salt. Pan-fry until mushrooms are browned and well reduced, then remove from pan and set aside.

» Add remaining butter to the pan, coating the bottom. Add onion, kale, and remaining salt. Sauté until onion is soft and beginning to brown, and kale is wilted.

» Add eggs and stir until cooked and scrambled into the vegetables. Remove from pan and toss with mushrooms.

» Reduce heat to medium-low. One at a time, place tortillas flat on the bottom of the pan. Cover half of the tortilla with half of the vegetable-egg mixture and half the cheese. Fold the tortilla in half and continue to cook, flipping once, until cheese is melted. Remove quesadilla and repeat with remaining tortilla and ingredients.

» Top with salsa to taste and serve.

CELERIAC BISQUE

SERVES 4

Celeriac is one of the less-understood vegetables at the market. Also known as celery root, it is in fact that: the root of a celery plant. Celeriac is a different varietal of celery than those grown for the stems, however—it's not much to look at from above, but impressive below the surface!

» Melt butter in a soup pot over medium heat. Add onion and salt. Sauté until onion softens and becomes fragrant, about 5 minutes.

» Add celeriac, potato, broth, and thyme. Increase heat to medium-high and simmer until vegetables are soft, about 45 minutes. Remove from heat.

» Either purée the soup in the pot with a stick blender, or transfer in batches to a stand blender, purée, and return to a clean pot. Return to medium heat.

» Add cream to soup and warm, stirring often, for 5 minutes. Add pepper to taste, stir, and serve.

INGREDIENTS

1/4 cup butter

1 large onion, diced

1 teaspoon salt

2 pounds (907 grams) celeriac, peeled, trimmed, and tender parts cut into bite-sized pieces

1 large potato, peeled and cut into bite-sized pieces

4 cups chicken or vegetable broth

1 tablespoon minced fresh thyme

1 cup whipping cream

pepper to taste

VIETNAMESE CARROT SALAD

SERVES 2

This bit of crunchy, spicy freshness packs well for a work lunch and is just what I need at lunchtime to power me up for the afternoon.

» Combine carrots and peanuts in a mixing bowl and toss to combine. Set aside.

» Combine lime juice, soy sauce, sugar, and jalapeño (if using) in a small bowl and whisk to combine.

» Pour dressing over carrot mixture and toss well. Allow salad to sit for five minutes, toss again, and serve.

INGREDIENTS

2 cups grated carrots

1/2 cup chopped peanuts

3 tablespoons lime juice

1 teaspoon soy sauce

1 teaspoon white sugar

1 jalapeño, seeded and minced (optional)

HOT PEPPER POT ROAST

SERVES 8

Bags of dried hot peppers are one of the many winter treasures that Rumtopf Farm (page 83) brings to the market. Crush them into a ground powder or use them in larger pieces to flavour a dish such as this roast.

» Preheat oven to 325°F (165°C).

» Season pot roast pieces with pepper and 1 1/2 teaspoons salt. Heat oil in a Dutch oven over medium-high heat, then add the pot roast pieces. Brown meat on all sides. Remove Dutch oven from heat.

» Add all remaining ingredients to Dutch oven and stir to combine.

» Bake, covered, until meat is tender, about 2 1/2 hours. Serve hot.

INGREDIENTS

1 beef pot roast, 2 1/2–3 pounds (1–1.4 kilograms), cut into large pieces

2 teaspoons black pepper

2 teaspoons salt, divided

2 tablespoons extra-virgin olive oil

2 medium onions, diced

3 garlic cloves, minced or pressed

1/4 cup tomato paste

1–2 tablespoons dried hot peppers, to taste

1 teaspoon dried thyme

1 cup beef broth

1 pound (454 grams) potatoes, peeled and chopped

1 pound (454 grams) carrots, peeled and chopped

1 tablespoon lemon juice

ROASTED HAZELNUT MAPLE TARTS

MAKES 12 TARTS

I'm pretty sure it's illegal to publish a book about food in Nova Scotia without paying homage at least once to maple syrup. Here it pairs beautifully with crunchy hazelnuts.

FOR THE TART SHELLS:

» In a large bowl, combine flour, powdered sugar, cinnamon, and salt. Whisk well.

» Add butter and water and combine with cold hands or a pastry blender until dough has the consistency of coarse bread crumbs.

» Wrap dough in plastic and transfer to the refrigerator for at least 1 hour (and no longer than 24 hours).

» When ready to continue, preheat oven to 375°F (190°C). Butter a muffin tin and set aside.

» Lightly flour a clean surface and roll chilled dough out to a roughly 5 mm thickness. Using a round cookie cutter or jar, cut out rounds slightly larger than the bottoms of the muffin tin. Gently press rounds into the bottom of each cup. Cover and chill in freezer while preparing the filling.

Continued on next page...

INGREDIENTS

For the tart shells:

1 1/4 cups all-purpose flour

1 tablespoon powdered sugar

1 teaspoon ground cinnamon

1/4 teaspoon salt

1/2 cup butter, cold and finely diced

3 tablespoons cold water

For the filling:

1/4 cup butter, room temperature

2/3 cup brown sugar

1/2 cup maple syrup

1 tablespoon vanilla extract

2 large eggs, lightly beaten

1 tablespoon all-purpose flour

2/3 cup chopped hazelnuts

FOR THE FILLING:

» Cream butter and brown sugar together until smooth and lightened in colour. Add maple syrup. Cream until well combined.

» Add vanilla and eggs and beat until well combined. Add flour slowly while stirring. Mix well and set aside.

» In a dry pan over medium heat, toast hazelnut pieces lightly while stirring constantly until nuts are fragrant and beginning to brown, about 2–3 minutes.

» Divide hazelnut pieces evenly between the cups, then pour the filling mixture over them, evenly dividing between cups.

» Bake for 20 minutes.

» Remove tarts from oven and allow to cool in the tin before serving.

APRIL

APPLE SPICE PANCAKES

SERVES 2–3

Nova Scotia is an apple province, and I'm rarely more grateful for that fact than in April, when it feels like we've been waiting forever for the good weather (and it's still not here yet!). At least we have high quality local fruit ready to add some sweetness to our day.

INGREDIENTS

1 1/2 cups rolled oats

1 pinch salt

1/2 teaspoon baking powder

1 tablespoon brown sugar

1 teaspoon ground cinnamon

1 teaspoon ground nutmeg

2 tablespoons ground almonds

1 egg

1 cup whole milk

1 teaspoon vanilla extract (or so—I believe in measuring vanilla with your heart)

2 medium apples, peeled, cored, and diced

butter for frying

» Place oats in a blender or food processor and blend until oats have the consistency of flour, 1–2 minutes.

» Combine oat flour, salt, baking powder, brown sugar, cinnamon, nutmeg, and ground almonds in a mixing bowl and whisk to combine.

» In a second mixing bowl, combine egg, milk, and vanilla extract and beat well.

» Add dry ingredients to wet ingredients and mix until just blended. Add apples and fold to combine.

» Heat a large frying pan over medium heat. Melt butter evenly across bottom of pan, then pour pancake batter, about 1/4 cup per pancake. When batter starts to bubble, flip pancakes. Cook evenly until browned on each side. Serve immediately.

ROMANO BEAN CABBAGE SOUP

SERVES 4

This soup works well with nearly any bean you like. I'm a fan of Jacob's Cattle beans, a soft-skinned bean grown here in the Maritimes.

» Combine olive oil, onion, and salt in a stockpot. Sauté on medium-low heat, stirring occasionally, until onion is soft, about 10 minutes.

» Add cabbage, broth, and beans and bring the soup to a simmer. Simmer until cabbage is cooked and tender, about 20 minutes.

» Add Romano and pepper and stir until cheese is melted. Serve immediately.

INGREDIENTS

2 tablespoons extra-virgin olive oil

1 onion, minced

1/2 teaspoon salt

1/2 medium cabbage, any varietal, cored and finely sliced

4 cups chicken or vegetable broth

2 cups cooked beans, any varietal

1 cup grated Romano cheese

pepper to taste

HADDOCK WITH BROWNED BUTTER WINE SAUCE

SERVES 2

Haddock is our go-to fish these days, as it is for many of our neighbours—although we could substitute any similar white fish in this dish. We use this recipe when we're pretending to be fancy.

INGREDIENTS

For the haddock:

1 pound (454 grams) fresh haddock fillets, patted dry

juice of 1 lemon

salt and pepper to taste

1/4 cup all-purpose flour

3 tablespoons butter

1 teaspoon dried thyme

For the sauce:

2 tablespoons butter

1 teaspoon dried thyme

1/2 cup dry white wine

1/2 cup heavy cream

zest of 1 lemon

FOR THE FILLETS:

» Place the fillets in a single layer on a tray or baking sheet, then squeeze the lemon juice over them evenly. Salt and pepper generously.

» Place flour in a bowl and lightly dredge each fillet, returning to the baking sheet.

» Heat a sauté pan over medium heat. Add butter and swirl to coat the bottom of the pan.

» Add the floured fillets and cook until golden brown, 3–5 minutes per side. Sprinkle dried thyme evenly onto the fillets halfway through.

» Return fillets to baking sheet and cover to keep warm.

Continued on next page...

» Add butter to pan used to cook fish and cook on medium heat until butter begins to brown and emit a nutty odour.

» Add the thyme and wine and increase the heat to medium-high.

» Cook the sauce, stirring, until wine reduces by half, about 10 minutes.

» Reduce heat to low and add cream. Cook, stirring, until sauce thickens slightly, 3–5 minutes. Remove from heat.

» Spoon hot sauce over fillets, then top with a sprinkle of lemon zest. Serve immediately.

OK SEA SALT

Onya Hogan-Finlay and Kim Kelly moved to Nova Scotia from Los Angeles in 2019. With a desire to root themselves in a rural community, they bought a home in the LaHave Islands. Inspired by their location, they created a business harvesting salt from the ocean, which they blend with locally-foraged wild ingredients such as beach rose, garlic scapes, spruce tips, lovage, blueberries, and cranberries. They brought their products to the LFM for the first time in 2022.

Their salts are versatile and can be used on a wide range of foods as finishing salts, with the berry salts carrying a tang of acid rather than prominent berry flavours. "A carrot ginger soup with purple blueberry salt on top is such a crowd pleaser… We really like contrasting colours. The spruce tips are fantastic on salads," says Onya. Several salts work beautifully on roasted vegetables, or to rim cocktail glasses.

Close to home, the LFM is a valuable market for them as eco-conscious business owners working toward a goal of net-zero business emissions. The blend of locals and summer tourists at the market is also a good fit for OK Sea Salt, because who can resist a perfect bag of salt as a souvenir from Nova Scotia? And, like all the vendors, they appreciate the deep sense of community at the market—they organized Petite Queer Pride, the first Pride event in Petite Rivière, with generous contributions from farmers at the LFM to fill lunch boxes and offer door prizes.

"It's wonderful to meet these folks who've been at it for years, and then there's also a lot of younger folks," Onya says of the vendors at the market. "So there's lots of learning together and sharing of advice."

JUNIPER HAM CALZONI

SERVES 8

This recipe is a slight variation on my favourite childhood dinner. A hearty cold-weather dish that warms up your kitchen as well as your tum, my mother used to make it without complaint for my birthday in July every year. That's a mother's love for you. (Thanks, Mom!)

At the Lunenburg Farmers' Market, you can find juniper ham for sale at the Webbersfood table. You could also use any sliced ham as a substitute.

» Place a rack in the middle of the oven and preheat to 450°F (230°C). Lightly grease a baking sheet with olive oil and set aside.

» In a mixing bowl, thoroughly combine ricotta, mozzarella, egg, juniper ham, and cooked greens.

» Divide pizza dough into 8 equal pieces. Flatten and roll each piece into a 6-inch round. Place a heaping spoonful of filling in the middle of each round. Moisten edges with water, fold in half, and pinch to seal. Place each calzone on the prepared baking sheet. Let rest 10 minutes, then make 2 short slashes on top of each calzone with a sharp knife.

» Bake until crusts are evenly browned, about 20 minutes. Remove from oven and immediately brush lightly with olive oil and sprinkle with finishing salt. Allow to cool for 10 minutes before serving. Calzoni can be served warm or cold.

INGREDIENTS

1 tablespoon extra-virgin olive oil, plus extra for baking sheet

1 cup (8 ounces) ricotta cheese

3/4 cup (6 ounces) shredded mozzarella cheese

1 egg

6 ounces (28 grams) juniper ham, finely diced

1 large bag spinach or other winter green to taste, cooked, drained, squeezed dry, and chopped

1 3/4 pounds (800 grams) pizza dough (enough for 2 pizzas), bought or homemade

plain or flavoured finishing salt, such as OK Sea Salt (page 41), to taste

CHOCOLATE RUM BITES

MAKES 24

Ironworks rum is valuable stuff—we hoard it to showcase in recipes (such as this one) that allow its quality to shine.

INGREDIENTS

1 teaspoon instant coffee granules

1/4 cup Ironworks rum

1/2 cup (4 ounces) cream cheese, room temperature

1 cup powdered sugar

1 cup almond flour

3 ounces (85 grams) unsweetened chocolate, melted

1/2 cup chocolate sprinkles (optional)

» Combine coffee granules and rum in a small pot. Heat on low, stirring until granules dissolve fully. Remove from heat.

» Add cream cheese, powdered sugar, and almond flour to rum mixture and stir until well combined. Add melted chocolate and stir to combine again.

» Transfer pot to the refrigerator and cool for 1 hour.

» Shape mixture into bite-sized balls. Roll each ball in sprinkles, if using. Store in a tightly-lidded container in the refrigerator, separating layers with wax paper.

MAY

RHUBARB WALNUT BREAD

SERVES 6

Colourful stalks of rhubarb are a sight for sore eyes at this time of year. Celebrate them in this sweet and spicy quick bread!

INGREDIENTS

2/3 cup melted butter, plus extra for loaf pan

1 1/2 cups brown sugar

1 egg

1 cup buttermilk

2 1/2 cups all-purpose flour

1 teaspoon baking soda

1/2 teaspoon salt

1 1/2 teaspoons ground cardamom

2 cups diced rhubarb

1/2 cup minced candied ginger

3/4 cup chopped walnuts

» Preheat oven to 350°F (177°C). Generously butter a loaf pan and set aside.

» Combine butter, brown sugar, egg, and buttermilk in a mixing bowl. Whisk until thoroughly combined.

» In a second bowl, combine flour, baking soda, salt, and cardamom. Whisk to combine.

» Add dry ingredients to wet ingredients and mix until just combined. Add diced rhubarb, candied ginger, and walnuts. Stir to distribute pieces evenly, then transfer to the prepared loaf pan.

» Bake until a knife inserted in the middle comes out clean, about 1 hour. Allow bread to cool in the pan before serving.

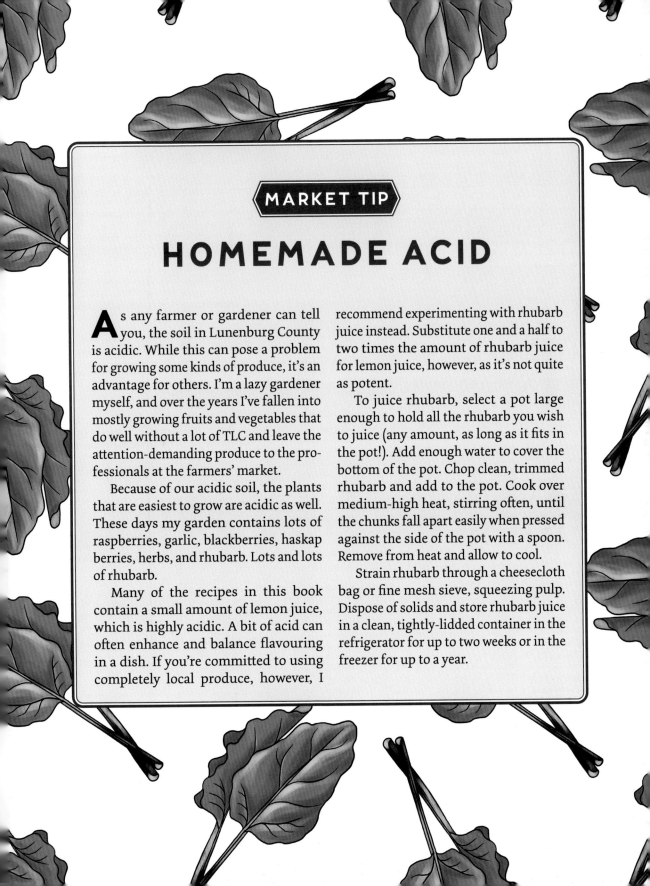

HOMEMADE ACID

As any farmer or gardener can tell you, the soil in Lunenburg County is acidic. While this can pose a problem for growing some kinds of produce, it's an advantage for others. I'm a lazy gardener myself, and over the years I've fallen into mostly growing fruits and vegetables that do well without a lot of TLC and leave the attention-demanding produce to the professionals at the farmers' market.

Because of our acidic soil, the plants that are easiest to grow are acidic as well. These days my garden contains lots of raspberries, garlic, blackberries, haskap berries, herbs, and rhubarb. Lots and lots of rhubarb.

Many of the recipes in this book contain a small amount of lemon juice, which is highly acidic. A bit of acid can often enhance and balance flavouring in a dish. If you're committed to using completely local produce, however, I recommend experimenting with rhubarb juice instead. Substitute one and a half to two times the amount of rhubarb juice for lemon juice, however, as it's not quite as potent.

To juice rhubarb, select a pot large enough to hold all the rhubarb you wish to juice (any amount, as long as it fits in the pot!). Add enough water to cover the bottom of the pot. Chop clean, trimmed rhubarb and add to the pot. Cook over medium-high heat, stirring often, until the chunks fall apart easily when pressed against the side of the pot with a spoon. Remove from heat and allow to cool.

Strain rhubarb through a cheesecloth bag or fine mesh sieve, squeezing pulp. Dispose of solids and store rhubarb juice in a clean, tightly-lidded container in the refrigerator for up to two weeks or in the freezer for up to a year.

GINGER RADISH FRIDGE PICKLES

MAKES 1 LITRE

If you'd like to try substituting rhubarb juice for the acid in this recipe (see Homemade Acid, page 49), simply use 2 cups of rhubarb juice instead of 1 cup of lemon juice or vinegar and omit the 1 cup of water.

INGREDIENTS

2 tablespoons dried hot chili flakes (optional)

one 1-inch chunk ginger, peeled and thinly sliced

2 tablespoons salt

1 cup water

1 cup lemon juice or rice vinegar

1/4 cup sugar

2 cups sliced radishes

» Combine all ingredients except sliced radishes in a pot and bring to a simmer over medium heat. Simmer for 5 minutes.

» Pack sliced radishes into a container. Carefully add pickling mixture to sliced radishes, making sure that all slices are completely covered.

» Cover tightly and store in the refrigerator for at least 1 week before eating. Pickles will keep up to 6 weeks in the refrigerator.

SPRING GREEN SOUP

SERVES 6–8

This recipe includes a little bit of everything that's peeking up in farmers' fields and greenhouses as we swing into spring! For the spring greens, consider any combination of mustard greens, Asian greens, Swiss chard, radish greens, young dandelion greens, or spinach.

» Heat broth over medium-high heat until simmering, then add orzo, greens, and radishes. Cook at a simmer, stirring occasionally, until orzo is cooked through, about 7 minutes.

» Add green garlic and chicken (if using), turn heat to medium, and cook another 2 minutes. Add salt and pepper to taste and serve.

INGREDIENTS

8 cups chicken or vegetable broth

3/4 cup orzo

8 cups packed chopped spring greens

1 cup cleaned chopped radishes (increase to 3 cups if not using chicken)

1/4 cup minced green garlic

1 pound (454 grams) cooked shredded chicken (optional)

salt and pepper to taste

AMINA'S SYRIAN KITCHEN

Ironically, farmers' market day is the time of the week I am least likely to cook! Usually I spend any free time I have prepping my vegetables for meals in the coming days—so it's perfect that the best prepared food I know of also comes from the LFM.

Amina Alouch learned about the LFM from fellow Chester resident Laura Mulrooney—well-known to market customers as the owner of Julien's Bakery, a long-lived Chester institution and cornerstone of the market before the well-deserved retirement of Julien and Laura in 2022.

Amina, her husband, Rayad, and their three children came to Nova Scotia through The Starfish Refugee Project, settling in Chester in 2019. They started their business using family recipes originating in Syria and Turkey. These include tabbouleh, fatayer (a traditional spinach-filled bread, although Amina offers other flavours as well), a variety of hummuses, samosas, and much, much more. Her food can also be found at locations in Chester and Bridgewater, and the family hopes to expand to their own commercial space in the future.

Her experience at the LFM has been strongly positive. "Very nice people," she assures me with a twinkling smile, as she slips a little extra something in my bag. They are, and she fits in perfectly.

MOROCCAN LAMB STEW

SERVES 6-8

This spiced stew with a Nova Scotian twist is a warming dish that pairs well with potatoes, rice, quinoa, or couscous.

» Combine stew meat, salt, and pepper in a mixing bowl and toss to coat.

» Heat a large soup pot or Dutch oven over medium-high heat and add olive oil.

» Add meat to pot and turn every few minutes until seared on all sides, about 15 minutes.

» Add all other ingredients and stir well. Bring to a boil, then reduce to a simmer and cook, stirring occasionally, for 1 hour. Remove from heat, allow to cool slightly, and serve.

INGREDIENTS

2 pounds (907 grams) lamb stew meat

1 tablespoon salt

1 teaspoon ground black pepper

2 tablespoons extra-virgin olive oil

1 large onion, diced

3 garlic cloves, minced or pressed

2 tablespoons fresh minced ginger

3 carrots, peeled and sliced

3 cups cooked chickpeas

6 cups beef broth

1 tablespoon ground cumin

1 tablespoon ground coriander

1 pinch ground cinnamon

1/2 cup dried apples, chopped

BOOZY ROOT BEER MILKSHAKE

SERVES 2

Over my decades in Lunenburg it's been a joy to watch several different distilleries develop unique local products, like the moonshine featured in this recipe. Feel free to vary the proportions of ice cream to liqueur to suit your preferences.

» Combine ice cream and liqueur in a blender and blend to combine. Pour into 2 glasses and top generously with whipped cream.

» If using the hard candy, secure in a freezer bag and crush with a rolling pin (or hammer, if you've got some issues to work out). Sprinkle whipped cream with crushed candy.

INGREDIENTS

3 cups vanilla ice cream

1/2 cup Still Fired Distilleries Root Beer Moonshine (or other market liqueur of your choice)

whipped cream

root beer–flavoured hard candy (optional)

JUNE

MARKET BREAKFAST SANDWICH

Serves 4

The biggest challenge I've had with homemade breakfast sandwiches has been getting them to hold together! One day it occurred to me that I could use the same trick I use for filled grilled cheese sandwiches, which is essentially to use two slices of cheese as a glue to hold the other ingredients in place.

» Using 1 tablespoon of butter per bun half, butter the insides of the bun, then line each half with a slice of cheese. Carefully add your fillings of choice and assemble sandwiches.

» Add roughly 2 tablespoons of butter to a pan, then gently press the sandwiches into the hot pan with a spatula until cheese is melted, about 3 minutes. Carefully flip sandwiches and repeat on the other side. Serve immediately.

INGREDIENTS

4 soft buns

8 tablespoons butter, plus extra for pan

8 slices cheese, any kind

any pre-cooked fillings you wish to use in your sandwich—sausage patties, bacon, omelet, fried egg, veggies, etc.

SEEDY STRAWBERRY SALAD

SERVES 4

Still have some juiced rhubarb? You can use it as a substitute for the balsamic vinegar in this recipe for an extra-local flavour (see Homemade Acid, page 49).

INGREDIENTS

3 cups baby spinach, loosely packed

2 cups washed and sliced strawberries

1/4 cup crushed walnut pieces

1/4 cup almond or walnut oil

2 tablespoons balsamic vinegar

1 tablespoon white sugar

2 teaspoons poppy seeds

» Combine baby spinach, strawberries, and walnut pieces in a serving bowl and toss lightly.

» In a smaller bowl, combine oil, balsamic vinegar, sugar, and poppy seeds and whisk together to form dressing.

» Pour dressing over salad and toss again. Serve immediately.

BOOZE

If you drink alcohol, flavouring spirits with local fruit is a great way to highlight the fruit flavours.

For most fruits, vodka is a good pairing, but some fruit flavours work better with another spirit. I recommend using tequila for strawberries, gin for rhubarb, and brandy for cherries or plums. To make your own flavoured drinks, simply cut up the fruit, place it in a clean jar with a tight-fitting lid, and cover with spirits. Add sugar to taste and store in a cool, dry place for at least two weeks. Give the jar a shake or stir every day or so.

After two weeks, strain the liquid through a fine mesh strainer or cheesecloth bag, squeezing the leftover pulp to get out any remaining juice. Store in a clean bottle or jar and enjoy at your leisure!

GREEK HORTA

SERVES 4 AS A SIDE DISH

Did you impulse-buy a lot of greens at the market? This is the perfect recipe to use any leftover greens that are starting to wilt, as well as any handfuls of greens from the garden. This simple dish dates back to ancient Greece and the tradition of combining varied seasonal greens throughout the year. For the greens, try any combination of Swiss chard, kale, spinach, arugula, mustard greens, radish greens, turnip greens, carrot greens, lamb's quarters, or dandelion greens.

» Combine water and salt in a large pot with a tight lid. Bring to a boil, then add greens. Cover and lower heat to a simmer. Cook until thickest greens are cooked through and soft, roughly 20 minutes, stirring occasionally.

» Drain, add olive oil, and toss.

» Serve horta as a side dish, add to pasta sauce, use as pizza topping, or mince and mix it with a soft cheese for sandwich filling or bagel topping.

INGREDIENTS

1 cup water

1/2 teaspoon salt

4 cups washed and roughly chopped greens, well packed

1/4 cup extra-virgin olive oil

5-WAY ROAST CHICKEN

EACH CHICKEN SERVES 4

This is one of my favourite easy cook-ahead recipes. I like to roast a chicken or two from Out to Pasture Farm (page 75) on the weekend, then use the meat in at least a couple of dinners throughout the week.

» Preheat oven to 350°F (177°C) and place a rack just under the halfway point of the oven. Generously butter a large baking pan. If included, remove the neck, giblets, and truss from the chicken. Place the chicken in the pan and drizzle melted butter over the entire bird. Season liberally with salt and pepper.

» Place chopped onion and garlic inside the body cavity.

» Bake until an instant thermometer inserted into the thickest part of the thigh reads 165°F (75°C), approximately 30-60 minutes. Remove chicken and allow to cool, then strip the carcass of the meat. Chop meat roughly and refrigerate. Reserve the carcass for stock or compost.

» Way One: serve chopped chicken with gravy and mashed potatoes.

» Way Two: toss chopped chicken with olive oil and taco seasoning, then use in tacos or as a topping for nachos.

» Way Three: toss chopped chicken with cooked pasta, lemon juice, black pepper, and grated Parmesan.

» Way Four: mince chicken and blend with soft cheese and herbs—such as goat cheese and fresh thyme, or cotija and cilantro—as a sandwich filling.

» Way Five: shred chicken into a soup or stew.

INGREDIENTS

1 whole chicken, 2-3 pounds (1-1.3 kilograms)

2 tablespoons butter, melted, plus extra for pan

salt and pepper to taste

1 onion, chopped

4 cloves garlic, chopped

HONEY TAFFY

MAKES 2–3 DOZEN PIECES OF TAFFY

Honey is one of my very favourite ways to savour the terroirs and flavours of Nova Scotia. As the bees gather pollen from native plants, they construct a sweet, elemental representation of what grows across their territory. For a fuller appreciation of this subtle but profound taste of place, omit the cinnamon and vanilla.

INGREDIENTS

cooking spray

1 1/2 cups honey

2 teaspoons ground cinnamon

2 teaspoons vanilla extract

» Line a rimmed baking sheet with parchment paper and spray evenly with cooking spray. Set aside.

» Combine honey, cinnamon, and vanilla in a large saucepan. Cook on medium-low heat, uncovered, until honey begins to bubble, 8–10 minutes. Continue cooking for another 10 minutes or until a candy thermometer reads 280°F (140°C).

» Transfer honey mixture to prepared baking sheet and spread out evenly with a spatula. Allow to rest until still warm but comfortable to touch, about 20 minutes.

» Lightly coat hands with cooking spray. Shape honey mixture into a ball. Stretch out into a rope, then double the rope back on itself. Repeat, pulling and folding the rope of taffy until the colour lightens, about 5 minutes. Spray rope lightly with cooking spray and cover with plastic wrap. Refrigerate for 15 minutes.

» Roll out taffy in thin ropes, cutting off bite-sized pieces. Wrap each piece in wax paper.

JULY

RED PEPPER DIP

SERVES 4

Bell peppers and cherry tomatoes really capture the taste of summer for me—never better than in this easy dip. Great for snacking on hot-weather days!

» Toss pepper halves with olive oil, minced rosemary, and salt. Broil until tender, 2–3 minutes per side. Cool, then finely dice.

» Combine diced peppers, garlic, tomatoes, feta, and soft cheese and mix until well blended. Serve with toasted pita or pita chips.

INGREDIENTS

3–4 medium red bell peppers, halved and seeded

1 tablespoon extra-virgin olive oil

1/2 teaspoon salt

1 teaspoon minced fresh rosemary

3 cloves garlic, minced or pressed

10 cherry tomatoes, quartered

1 cup crumbled feta cheese

1 cup goat cheese or cream cheese

ROAST CHERRY BREAKFAST PANNA COTTA

SERVES 3

Panna cotta's a lovely dish when you have time to make it. If you don't, feel free to skip the gelée, or simply roast your cherries and plop them on yogurt for a still-sumptuous breakfast.

INGREDIENTS

For the panna cotta:

2 tablespoons water

1 1/2 teaspoons gelatin

1/2 cup whipping cream

1 cup milk

1/4 cup sugar

1 teaspoon vanilla extract

For the gelée:

3/4 cup water

1 tablespoon gelatin

juice from 6 cherries

For the topping:

1 cup cherries, halved and pitted

1 tablespoon brown sugar

1 tablespoon lemon juice

zest of 1 lemon

FOR THE PANNA COTTA:

» Place water in a small bowl and sprinkle gelatin on top. Allow to bloom for 5 minutes.

» In the meantime, combine cream, milk, sugar, and vanilla in a pot. Bring to a simmer over medium heat, stirring often, until sugar dissolves and mixture is hot. Remove from heat and whisk in the gelatin mixture. Transfer panna cotta to 3 serving dishes, cover with plastic wrap, and refrigerate overnight.

FOR THE GELÉE (THE NEXT DAY):

» Place water in a small bowl and sprinkle gelatin on top. Allow to bloom for 5 minutes.

» Add cherry juice and stir. Pour gelée over top of panna cottas, dividing equally. Refrigerate until set, about 2 hours.

FOR THE TOPPING:

» When ready to continue, preheat oven to 400°F (200°C). Line a baking pan with parchment paper.

» Combine cherries, brown sugar, and lemon juice in a bowl, toss, and transfer to prepared pan. Bake for 20 minutes. Cool completely before assembling.

» Spoon cherry mixture over top of panna cottas, dividing equally. Top each with a sprinkle of lemon zest. Serve.

ZUCCHINI FRIES

SERVES 2

When my son was little, he'd eat anything if it was a kind of fry. Thus began our journey into veggie fries. This was a house favourite (can't recommend the carrot fries, though).

» Preheat oven to 425°F (220°C). Line a baking sheet with parchment paper and set aside.

» Slice off both ends of the zucchini and cut them into fourths lengthwise. Set aside.

» Combine bread crumbs, Parmesan, Italian seasoning, salt, and pepper in a bowl. Whisk until thoroughly combined.

» In a separate bowl, whisk the eggs.

» Dip zucchini fries in egg, then coat with bread-crumb mixture. Place on prepared baking sheet. Bake for 20 minutes, flipping fries halfway through. Allow to cool slightly, then serve.

INGREDIENTS

3 medium zucchini

1 cup bread crumbs (panko or homemade)

1/2 cup grated Parmesan cheese

1 teaspoon Italian seasoning

1/2 teaspoon salt

1/2 teaspoon pepper

2 eggs

OUT TO PASTURE FARM

One of the highlights of the market for me has always been meat from Kevin Veinotte's Out to Pasture Farm. A seventh-generation farmer from West Northfield, Kevin takes advantage of the ideal grass-growing climate in Nova Scotia to farm and expertly finish grass-fed beef for his customers.

The Belted Galloways and Lowline Angus he tends are born on the farm and, unlike most beef cattle, are able to live every day of their lives there, as Kevin has his own processing facility. The same is true for the free-range chickens, turkeys, and lambs he sells as well. "The animals don't leave the farm, they aren't stressed, and the meat's not in and out of coolers. We've always stood by 'if we didn't grow it, we won't sell it.' That's one of the reasons the Lunenburg [Farmers'] Market is successful—you're dealing with the farmer that grew it," Kevin says.

A twenty-two-year veteran of LFM, Kevin is grateful to the customers who have stood by him over the years, especially as he learned to cut beef. "One lady schooled me on the proper way to cut a standing prime rib roast," he recalls. "Our customers are as faithful as can be."

SHORT RIB TACOS

SERVES 2

A touch of cocoa adds richness to this recipe, just as it does with a pot of chili.

INGREDIENTS

2 tablespoons extra-virgin olive oil

6 bone-in beef short ribs

salt and pepper to taste

2 cloves garlic, minced or pressed

1 small onion, diced

1 tablespoon baking cocoa

1 1/2 cups tomato sauce

1 1/2 cups beef broth

» Preheat oven to 325°F (165°C). Heat olive oil over medium-high heat in a cast iron pan. Generously season ribs with salt and pepper. Brown ribs in cast iron pan in batches, then remove from pan.

» Add garlic and onion to the same pan and cook, stirring frequently, for 5 minutes. Add cocoa, tomato sauce, and beef broth. Bring to a simmer, scraping to release any bits stuck to the bottom of the pan.

» Return ribs to pan, cover, and transfer to oven. Bake until meat is tender, about 3 hours. Remove from oven and allow to cool. Remove ribs and shred meat, discarding bones.

» Skim any fat from the surface of the remaining liquid, then return meat to the pan and reheat over medium heat before serving.

» Serve with warmed tortillas, shredded cheese, your favourite vegetables, and salsa.

NO-CHURN RASPBERRY ICE CREAM

SERVES 4

Raspberries love the acidic soil here in Nova Scotia. This easy ice cream makes loving them back inevitable.

» Place a clean loaf pan or similar baking pan in the freezer.

» Place raspberries in a fine mesh or cheesecloth bag. With clean hands, squeeze bag to release juice into a large mixing bowl. Continue to squeeze until as much juice as possible is expressed.

» Add vanilla, salt, and sweetened condensed milk to raspberry juice. Whisk to combine.

» In a separate bowl, using a mixer, whip the whipping cream on medium-high speed until firm peaks form. Add whipped cream to raspberry mixture gradually, gently folding until just combined.

» Transfer mixture to chilled pan and cover. Freeze until solid, about 5 hours.

INGREDIENTS

1 pint (about 2 cups) raspberries

2 teaspoons vanilla extract

1 pinch salt

one 300-ml can sweetened condensed milk

2 cups whipping cream

AUGUST

SAVE IT

Eating fresh seasonal food is great—when the food you want to eat is in season! Luckily, it's not that difficult to preserve market produce for a snowy day. While canning is traditional, the easiest and most nutritious way to preserve produce is to freeze it.

To maximize the taste of frozen produce, it's best to blanch it, or cook it very slightly, first. This process stops the enzymatic processes inside the tissues and helps keep them fresh. Blanching vegetables is a quick process:

Wash and trim pieces to the size you want them (similar to commercially-frozen vegetables). Fill a large pan half-full of ice-cold water and set aside.

Fill a large stockpot with enough water to cover your vegetables and bring it to a boil over high heat. Add vegetables and boil for 2–8 minutes, depending on the nature of the vegetables (see chart at right).

At the end of the blanching time, quickly drain the vegetables and transfer them to the ice water to stop the cooking process. Allow to sit for one minute,

then drain vegetables and shake off excess water or pat dry.

Label and date freezer bags or containers and transfer vegetables to them. Freeze. Use within 6 months.

VEGETABLE BLANCHING TIMES	
Asparagus	2–3 minutes
Broccoli	3 minutes
Brussels sprouts	4 minutes
Cauliflower	3 minutes
Celery	3 minutes
Corn on the cob	8 minutes
Corn kernels	4 minutes
Eggplant	4 minutes
Green beans	3 minutes
Peas	2 minutes
Peppers	3 minutes
Spinach and other leafy greens	2 minutes
Sunchokes (Jerusalem artichokes)	4 minutes
Zucchini	3 minutes

MARKET VEGGIE CUPS

MAKES 12 CUPS

Make these ahead for lunches throughout the week and enjoy them rewarmed or at room temperature.

INGREDIENTS

1 pound (454 grams) pizza dough

2 tablespoons extra-virgin olive oil, plus extra to grease muffin tin

2 large sweet peppers, chopped

1 onion, finely chopped

1 cup chopped mushrooms

1 teaspoon salt

1/2 cup pesto

1/4 cup grated cheese, any kind

» Preheat oven to 350°F (177°C). Lightly grease a 12-cup muffin tin with extra-virgin olive oil.

» Line 12 muffin cups with a thin layer of pizza dough, shaping a cup that extends at least 2/3 of the way up the sides. Bake for 10 minutes. Keep oven on, but set dough cups aside to cool slightly. If they have puffed up very much, press the dough flat with the back of a spoon.

» In the meantime, heat olive oil in a sauté pan over medium heat. Add chopped peppers, onion, mushrooms, and salt. Sauté until vegetables are soft and fragrant, about 10 minutes.

» Line the inside of the cups with pesto, then distribute sautéed vegetables among the cups. Top with cheese and return to oven.

» Back until pastry is golden brown, another 15–20 minutes. Cool for at least 10 minutes before removing from tin.

» Veggie cups will keep, wrapped in aluminum foil or plastic wrap, for up to 4 days in the refrigerator.

RUMTOPF FARM

Wanda and Michael Wolter first met at the agricultural college in Truro over forty years ago. A girl from Cape Breton and a boy from Heidelberg, Germany, both were excited about the future of farming. After finishing their degrees in Guelph, Ontario, they returned to Nova Scotia, eventually purchasing their farm in Conquerall Mills in 1983. Their neighbours brought an oxen team over to prepare a plot of their land, which then became a market garden. They were brand new to farmers' markets when they became founding members of the LFM.

Over the years they have become known for their wide variety of vegetables, introducing such delectable options as fennel, celeriac, and sunchokes. I first learned about lovage from Wanda—both the fact that you could use its leaves for seasoning similarly to celery leaves, and that you can turn the hollow stems of the plant into straws for Bloody Marys!

Long-time customers line up patiently at Rumtopf Farm's table to purchase their salad mixes, tender vegetables of all types, garlic, flavoured salts, and dried vegetable and pepper mixes for winter. Today, the Wolters' five adult children do most of the farming, so you're likely to meet some of them at the market.

When asked what she most likes to make with her own produce, Wanda sings the praises of multi-vegetable dishes. "I make a lot of coleslaw with celeriac, carrots, cabbage, onion, garlic, apple…" She's also a fan of ratatouille and roasted vegetables, both of which lend themselves to being made in big batches of freezable portions for easy meals any time.

After forty years of farmers' markets, Wanda only has good things to say about the experience: "It's just such a great way to do business, but it's so much more than business. There's so much socializing and trading of information and laughing and, you know, it's almost all pretty darn wonderful."

SPRING ONION PASTA

SERVES 4

Now that tomatoes, early onions, and garlic are available, it's time to capitalize on their fresh tastes in this simple but delectable pasta!

» Preheat oven to 400°F (200°C). Line a baking sheet with parchment paper and set aside.

» Combine tomato pieces, onion, garlic, olive oil, salt, pepper, and lemon juice in a mixing bowl and toss well. Transfer mixture to baking sheet and bake until vegetables are cooked through, about 30 minutes.

» In the meantime, cook pasta according to package directions.

» Combine cooked pasta, vegetable mixture, and Parmesan cheese in a serving bowl and toss to combine. Serve immediately.

INGREDIENTS

1 cup tomato pieces (halved cherry tomatoes and/or bite-sized chunks of larger tomatoes)

2 spring onions, chopped (both whites and greens)

6 cloves garlic, peeled and chopped

2 tablespoons extra-virgin olive oil

salt and pepper to taste

1 tablespoon lemon juice

9 ounces (250 grams) fusilli or other pasta

1 cup grated Parmesan cheese

SUMMERGREEN POTATOES

Serves 4

Tender new potatoes and peas need only a little coaxing to make a splendid meal in this quintessential summer recipe.

INGREDIENTS

2 pounds (907 grams) potatoes, cleaned and chopped into bite-sized pieces

1/4 cup extra-virgin olive oil, divided

salt and pepper to taste

1/4 cup chopped hazelnuts

1/2 cup chopped fresh mint

1/4 cup chopped fresh basil

1/4 cup grated Parmesan cheese

1 clove garlic, minced or pressed

2 tablespoons lemon juice

1 cup fresh shelled peas

» Preheat oven to 400°F (200°C). Toss potatoes with half the oil, salt, and pepper. Transfer to a baking sheet and roast until tender, 30–35 minutes.

» Meanwhile, toast the hazelnuts in a dry pan over medium heat, stirring frequently, until fragrant and beginning to brown, 2–3 minutes.

» Combine the remaining half of the oil, mint, basil, hazelnuts, Parmesan, garlic, and lemon juice and blend with a food processor or hand blender to create a rough paste.

» Toss roasted potatoes with peas and herbed Parmesan mixture and serve immediately, or refrigerate and serve cold.

HARVEST LASAGNA

SERVES 6

A little bit of everything to satisfy every inch of your palate!

» Preheat the oven to 425°F (220°C).

» Warm a large pan (9 x 12 or similar) over medium heat, then add olive oil and swirl to coat the bottom. Add carrots, bell pepper, zucchini, onion, garlic, and salt. Cook, stirring often, until veggies soften, 10–15 minutes.

» Add the spinach and continue to cook, stirring until spinach wilts. Remove pan from heat and set aside.

» Combine ricotta, Parmesan, and mozzarella in a bowl and stir well to combine.

» Spread a thin layer of tomato sauce on the bottom of a baking pan and cover with 3 sheets of lasagna. Cover lasagna sheets with 1/3 of the remaining tomato sauce, then 1/3 of the vegetable mixture, then 1/3 of cheese mixture. Repeat lasagna sheet/ tomato sauce/vegetable/cheese layering twice.

» Sprinkle red pepper flakes evenly on top of the lasagna. Cover the pan with foil and bake for 20 minutes, then uncover and bake until cheese browns, about another 10 minutes.

» Allow lasagna to cool for 15 minutes. While lasagna is cooling, mince fresh basil. Sprinkle minced basil evenly across the top and serve.

INGREDIENTS

2 tablespoons extra-virgin olive oil

1 cup shredded carrots

1 red bell pepper, diced

1 medium zucchini, diced

1 medium onion, diced

4 cloves garlic, minced or pressed

1 teaspoon salt

2 cups packed chopped spinach

1 cup ricotta cheese

3/4 cup grated Parmesan cheese

2 cups grated mozzarella cheese

2 cups tomato sauce

9 strips no-boil lasagna sheets

1/2 teaspoon red pepper flakes

1/2 cup packed fresh basil

BLUEBERRY CLAFOUTIS

SERVES 4

Clafoutis is a traditional French dessert made with whole, unpitted cherries. This blueberry version, based on a recipe by Julia Child, has all of its charm (with none of the pits)! If you're at the Lunenburg Farmers' Market, check out Michael Touesnard's table for an offering of delicious fresh blueberries.

» Place a rack in the middle of the oven and preheat to 350°F (177°C). Generously butter a medium (8-inch or 9-inch) round baking dish and set aside.

» Combine milk, sugar, eggs, vanilla, and salt in a bowl and beat well. Beat in flour, stirring to ensure there are no lumps.

» Distribute blueberries evenly on the bottom of the baking pan and cover with batter. Bake until a knife inserted in the centre comes out clean, about 50 minutes.

» Cool for 20 minutes, then sprinkle powdered sugar evenly across surface. Serve warm or cool.

INGREDIENTS

1 1/4 cups milk

2/3 cup sugar

3 eggs

1 tablespoon vanilla extract

1 pinch salt

1 cup flour

1 pint (about 2 cups) blueberries

1 tablespoon powdered sugar

SEPTEMBER

STONE SOUP

This isn't really a recipe—how could it be, when you can put anything you like in it? Rather, it's a method to make soup out of any assortment of produce. If you have a foundation of broth, oil (like butter or extra-virgin olive oil), salt, and pepper, you can make soup!

To start, cut your veggies into bite-sized pieces. For very firm vegetables such as potatoes, carrots, or celeriac, go even smaller. Next, heat your cooking oil of choice in the bottom of a soup pot—use about 1 tablespoon oil per 1 1/2 cups chopped vegetables.

Sauté the vegetables over medium-low heat until soft and fragrant. Add broth (any kind), about 1 1/2–2 cups to every cup of vegetables. Simmer, stirring occasionally, for 30 minutes.

At this point if you want a heartier soup, you can throw in a cup or two of cooked ingredients such as beans, chopped meat, rice, or pasta. You can also add some dairy for a creamy soup—cheese, sour cream, or yogurt.

Other things you can add to make it taste even better include garlic, fresh herbs, flavoured salt instead of plain, a dash of acid (lemon juice, wine, or rhubarb juice—see page 49), and spices. Soup doesn't have any stinkin' rules, so enjoy using your imagination!

MAGHREBI SHAKSHUKA

SERVES 4

It is believed that shakshuka originated in Tunisia, but the dish is well-known and commonly eaten throughout North Africa and the Middle East as well. Almost every region has formed their distinctive variety of shakshuka: in Egypt, eggs are usually scrambled and served in a sandwich, and in Israel it is often served with salty feta cheese on top. The consistency of the sauce and eggs also varies—the sauce can be thinner or thicker, while the eggs can be completely firm or soft.

To prepare this breakfast dish ahead of time, cook the stew, then refrigerate in meal-sized portions. To finish, simply reheat, add 1–2 eggs, cook until the whites are firm, and add a handful of chopped parsley if desired.

INGREDIENTS

1/4 cup extra-virgin olive oil, divided

2 green bell peppers, seeded and diced

2 large onions, diced

salt to taste

2 cups chopped fresh tomatoes

1 tablespoon cumin

1 tablespoon paprika (sweet, hot, or a combination)

8 eggs

1/2 cup finely chopped parsley (optional)

» Combine 2 tablespoons olive oil with diced green peppers in a sauté pan over medium-high heat. Cook until peppers just begin to soften, about 6 minutes. Remove sautéed peppers to a stockpot.

» Combine remaining 2 tablespoons olive oil with diced onions and salt in the hot sauté pan. Cook until softened and beginning to brown, 6–8 minutes. Transfer sautéed onions to stockpot.

» Add tomatoes, cumin, and paprika to stockpot. Cook stew over medium-low heat for 20 minutes, then make wells in the top of the stew for eggs. Carefully break eggs into wells, taking care not to break the yolks. Cover and continue to cook until egg whites are solid, 5–8 minutes.

» Remove stew from heat and garnish with chopped parsley if using. Serve immediately.

GARLIC AND GINGER KALE

SERVES 4

I like this dish best with a mixture of kales—poke around the market and try whichever ones grab your fancy!

» Heat peanut oil in a large sauté pan over medium-high heat. Add ginger, garlic, and kale. Sauté, stirring constantly, for about 7 minutes.

» Add broth, red pepper flakes, and teriyaki. Bring to a simmer and continue to cook another 4 minutes. Remove from heat and serve.

INGREDIENTS

1 tablespoon peanut oil

1 tablespoon minced fresh ginger

2 cloves garlic, minced or pressed

2 bunches kale, any kind, cleaned and chopped

1/4 cup vegetable or chicken broth

1 teaspoon red pepper flakes

1 tablespoon teriyaki or teriyaki shiitake sauce

MEXICAN CARNITAS

SERVES 6

I offer this recipe in fond memory of Kurt Wentzel, an expert butcher, meat vendor, friend, and long-time member of the LFM community. We all miss you, Kurt.

INGREDIENTS

2 pounds (907 grams) bone-less pork shoulder roast

2 teaspoons salt

2 tablespoons extra-virgin olive oil

4–5 cloves garlic, peeled and root end removed

1 tablespoon cumin

1 teaspoon ground oregano

2 whole hot peppers (any kind), fresh or dried, sliced lengthwise

» Chop shoulder roast into 4-inch cubes. Rub salt into meat, cover, and refrigerate for 1 hour or up to 24 hours.

» Preheat oven to 325°F (165°C).

» Heat a large cast iron pan over medium-high heat. Add olive oil, then carefully place meat in pan. Sear on all sides until nicely browned. Remove pan from heat and add garlic, cumin, ground oregano, and peppers. Add water until pan is just shy of completely filled. Transfer pan to oven.

» Braise, turning pork occasionally, until meat is very tender and comes apart when poked with a fork, about 3 1/2 hours.

» Using two forks, break meat down into shreds.

» Increase oven heat to 375°F (190°C). Return pan to oven for another 30 minutes.

» Allow to cool slightly before serving. Serve with rice, potatoes, or tortillas, or use as a burrito filling or nacho topping.

VANILLA CUPCAKES WITH BLACKBERRY FROSTING

MAKES 12 CUPCAKES

The dark sweetness of blackberries is a beguiling contrast to sweet, light vanilla cupcakes in this late summer treat.

» Preheat oven to 350°F (177°C). Line a cupcake pan with paper cups and set aside.

» Combine butter and sugar in a mixing bowl and beat until light and fluffy. Add eggs and vanilla extract and beat well. Add milk and beat again.

» In a second bowl, whisk flour and baking powder thoroughly.

» Add dry ingredients to wet ingredients slowly, mixing as you go until just combined. Pour batter into lined cupcake pan, filling each cup 2/3 full.

» Bake until a toothpick inserted in the middle of a cupcake comes out clean, about 18 minutes. Let cupcakes cool in the pans for 5 minutes, then transfer to a wire rack to finish cooling.

» While cupcakes are cooling, combine blackberries and lemon juice in a small saucepan over medium heat. Crush the blackberries against the side of the pan while stirring. Cook until blackberries soften, stirring often, about 5 minutes. Remove from heat and allow to cool.

» Strain the liquid through a fine mesh strainer or cheesecloth bag to remove solids.

» Combine blackberry liquid with all other frosting ingredients and beat until fluffy. Frost cupcakes as desired.

INGREDIENTS

For the cupcakes:

1 cup butter, room temperature

2 cups white sugar

4 eggs, room temperature

1 teaspoon vanilla extract

1 cup milk

2 3/4 cups all-purpose flour

1 tablespoon baking powder

For the frosting:

1 cup fresh blackberries

1 tablespoon lemon juice

1 cup butter, room temperature

4 cups powdered sugar

1/4 cup coffee cream or milk

1 teaspoon vanilla

1 pinch salt

MUSHROOM AND CARAMELIZED ONION PIE

SERVES 4

A walnut crust adds the perfect crunch to this late summer entrée.

INGREDIENTS

1/2 cup room temperature butter, divided

2 large onions, diced

1 teaspoon salt, divided

1 1/2 cups small walnut pieces

3 tablespoons melted butter

pepper to taste

4 cups diced mushrooms, any kind or a combination

4 cups spinach, chopped and lightly packed

2/3 cup ricotta cheese

2 tablespoons grated Parmesan cheese

» Combine 1/4 cup butter, onions, and 1/2 teaspoon salt in a large pan over medium-low heat. Cook, stirring occasionally, until onions are soft and brown, about 1 hour (but it will feel like 300 years).

» Preheat oven to 350°F (177°C).

» Pulverize walnut pieces in a food processor, or place in a freezer bag and crush with a rolling pin to make fine crumbs. Mix walnut crumbs and melted butter in a mixing bowl, adding remaining 1/2 teaspoon salt and pepper to taste. Press mixture into the bottom of a pie pan, distributing evenly. Bake until lightly browned, about 15 minutes. Allow to cool to room temperature.

» While crust is cooling, preheat oven to 375°F (190°C). Combine remaining 1/4 cup butter, mushrooms, and pepper to taste (I recommend peppering liberally) in a stockpot over medium-high heat. Cook, stirring often, until mushrooms have released their liquid and turned brown.

» Turn heat to medium-low, add spinach, stir, and cover. Continue to cook, removing lid to stir often, until spinach is wilted but still bright green, 5–7 minutes. Remove from heat, add caramelized onions and ricotta, and stir until evenly combined.

» Gently spread filling evenly over the cooled walnut crust. Sprinkle grated Parmesan evenly over the filling. Bake until Parmesan browns and filling is slightly bubbly, about 30 minutes. Allow to cool slightly before serving.

GARLIC
$12.00/lb

OCTOBER

SOIL MATES FARM

First-generation farmers Marena Thomson and Mykal Koloff met in 2015 and hit the ground running with their diversified mixed vegetable farm. In addition to the LFM and their Community Supported Agriculture (CSA) program, Soil Mates provides produce to many local restaurants, including Lincoln Street Food, Half Shell Oyster Bar, and The Kiwi Café.

"Our goal as farmers is to produce really delicious and nutritious food for our community and do so in an ecologically responsible manner," says Mykal, an East Chester native. "That was the guiding force between wanting to get into farming. I've always been interested in growing things, but part of it just came from awareness around the fragility of supply chains and global food production. Having resilience on a local level is really important for a community. Ultimately, having a farm just became our way to address that issue."

Like many farmers, Marena and Mykal love combining several vegetables into a single dish. One of their favourite things to do is lightly grill vegetables. "For instance I might take bok choy, broccolini, and Hakurei turnips in season with onions, and then lightly chop everything up," Mykal says. "Toss in a little bit of sesame oil, some tamari balsamic vinegar, a splash of maple syrup, or maybe a little bit of olive oil or something like that. Add garlic and just toss that up in a basket on the grill. It really brings out the flavours of all those vegetables."

Talking about their relationship with the LFM, he says, "The thing I like the most about the Lunenburg Farmers' Market is that it's centred around food, and many of the customers that come every week are really passionate about food—both about high quality and the power of local food and how that can build community. So I like the energy that brings to the market. A lot of people take an interest in how we do what we do. And I love having those kinds of conversations.

"I've found farming to be a really challenging and creative outlet. At the market vendors talk to each other as colleagues. We talk about what works and what doesn't, share tips. There's a lot of community around the market…and everyone's there because they're enthusiastic about what they do."

FALL BREAKFAST HASH

SERVES 4

Showcase fennel and butternut squash in this breakfast of autumnal champions. I recommend saving the fennel fronds for a salad.

» Preheat oven to 400°F (200°C).

» Heat an oven-safe pan (such as a cast iron pan) on medium heat. Add butter or olive oil and swirl to coat the bottom of the pan. Add fennel, onion, butternut squash, ginger, and salt. Cook, stirring often, for 10 minutes.

» Add vegetable broth and stir, scraping the bottom of the pan to release any stuck bits and to coat the vegetables with liquid. Continue to cook, stirring often, until squash is tender and cooked through, 5–10 minutes. Remove from heat.

» Break eggs over the top of the hash and add pepper to taste.

» Bake in preheated oven until eggs are cooked to taste, 5–10 minutes. Serve immediately.

INGREDIENTS

2 tablespoons butter or extra-virgin olive oil

1 bulb fennel, cleaned and sliced into bite-sized pieces, fronds removed

1 large onion, chopped

2 cups butternut squash, peeled, seeded, and cut into bite-sized pieces

2 teaspoons minced fresh ginger

1 teaspoon salt

1/4 cup vegetable broth

6 eggs

pepper to taste

GARLIC AND THYME ROASTED ROOT VEGGIES

SERVES 8

Use any root vegetables (such as carrots, celeriac, potatoes, and beets) that catch your fancy in this dish. If you're partial to carrots, try an assortment of colours for a roasted rainbow!

INGREDIENTS

2 pounds (907 grams) mixed fresh root vegetables, peeled and chopped into bite-sized pieces

4 cloves garlic, roughly chopped

1/4 cup olive oil

1 tablespoon minced fresh thyme

1 teaspoon salt

juice and zest of 1 small lemon

» Preheat oven to 400°F (200°C).

» In a mixing bowl, toss all ingredients together, then transfer to a large baking dish. Roast vegetables until they are tender, stirring occasionally, about 1 hour.

SAFFRON COD CHEEKS

SERVES 4

Cod cheeks are one of my favourite market buys. They have a meatier texture than fillets and deserve to be graced with delicate saffron. At the Lunenburg Farmers' Market, you can purchase them from The Fish Store.

» Combine olive oil, garlic, and salt over medium heat in a large skillet and sauté, stirring, for 1 minute.

» Add tomatoes, coriander, fenugreek, and saffron. Continue to cook, stirring, until mixture thickens slightly, 8–10 minutes.

» Layer cod cheeks over the top of the mixture and stir to combine. Cover tightly with lid and reduce heat to medium-low. Cook until cheeks are just cooked through, about 15 minutes. Serve with pasta or rice.

INGREDIENTS

2 tablespoons extra-virgin olive oil

4 cloves garlic, minced or pressed

1/2 teaspoon salt

2 cups canned or previously frozen diced tomatoes

1 teaspoon ground coriander

1 teaspoon ground fenugreek

1 pinch saffron threads

1 pound (454 grams) cod cheeks

COMPANY QUICHE

SERVES 4

For some reason, people seem extra impressed if you make your own quiche. This one-bowl recipe makes a crust and filling that separate from each other during the baking process.

INGREDIENTS

3/4 cup all-purpose flour

2 teaspoons baking soda

2 tablespoons cold butter, diced

1 generous pinch salt

2 cups milk

4 large eggs

1/4 cup butter, melted and slightly cooled

1 cup cooked, crumbled sausage (pork or vegetarian)

1 1/2 cups shredded cheddar cheese

1 fresh jalapeño, minced (optional)

» Preheat oven to 375°F (190°C). Generously butter a pie plate and set aside.

» Combine flour, baking soda, butter, and salt in a mixing bowl and quickly incorporate with a cold hand.

» Add milk, eggs, and melted butter and beat well (batter will be lumpy). Add sausage, cheese, and jalapeño (if using) and stir to combine. Transfer to the prepared pie pan.

» Bake until eggs are set and surface is golden brown, about 50 minutes.

FITCH LAKE FARM

"I didn't quite realize what I was getting into," Valerie Tanner says jokingly about marrying a farmer. LFM vendors since 1994, their family's main business focus is greenhouse plants, including bedding, hanging, and potted plants; herbs for transplant; and perennials.

An orchardist and market gardener, Greg Tanner also produces apples, pears, plums, and peaches in season, along with blueberries and blackberries. Valerie's especially proud of their crimson Gravenstein, Cox Queen, and Wolf River apples, the latter of which are so large that a single apple can make an entire pie.

Once Greg harvests the produce, Valerie gets to work turning them into a wide variety of jams and jellies, which are available for purchase at the market throughout the year along with whole fruit. Her bestseller is a hot pepper jelly, which she recommends using straight or mixing with barbecue sauce. Other recommendations include using apple jelly as a glaze on pork or chicken, or enjoying quince jelly with old cheddar on a cracker.

A veteran of several markets, Valerie waxes enthusiastic about the LFM. "The Lunenburg market is unique... There's a feeling of 'I'll do this in order to help the market' even if it doesn't necessarily benefit me. If a vendor needs help, people will jump in without being asked. If somebody wants something I don't have, I'll direct them to somebody who has what they want because I want their market experience to be good." Looking around the room any given Thursday morning, it's clear that the market community is happily thriving.

THANKFUL APPLE PIE

SERVES 8

To crush up the cookies for this recipe, place them in a freezer bag and crush them with a rolling pin or use your food processor. You can use any crispy cookie you like—for apple pie, I've used gingersnaps, almond cookies, and even peanut butter cookies with delicious success.

» Combine cookie crumbs and melted butter and work into an even dough by hand. Generously butter a pie pan. Pat crumb mixture firmly and evenly onto bottom and sides of pan. Refrigerate for at least 1 hour.

» Preheat oven to 375°F (190°C).

» Combine sugar, apples, cinnamon, ginger powder, nutmeg, cornstarch, and vanilla extract in a mixing bowl and toss well. Pour into prepared pie pan, then bake on a rack in the lower third of the oven until apples are softened and filling is bubbly, about 40 minutes. Cool, then serve.

INGREDIENTS

1 2/3 cup finely crushed cookie crumbs

1/4 cup melted butter, plus extra for pan

3/4 cup sugar

4 cups peeled diced apples, any kind

1 teaspoon cinnamon

1 teaspoon ginger powder

1 teaspoon nutmeg

1 tablespoon cornstarch

1 1/2 teaspoons vanilla extract

RULES OF THE ROAD

The market is a bustle of activity: vendors and customers getting to know each other and exchanging tips, children exploring, friends and neighbours connecting over coffee… community happening. I love being a part of it and hope you do, too! To help make it a great experience for everyone, I warmly recommend keeping the following guidelines in mind:

Pass with care. Just like a highway, the market has lanes of traffic to observe and be aware of. Some folks go slower or faster than others, and there's room for all of us.

Pull over to the shoulder before coming to a complete stop. See a friend you'd like to chat with for a minute or two? Lovely. Step aside and out of the traffic flow—then spill that tea.

Mind your blind spot and be aware of commuters. The crowd at the market is a peculiar mix of people who have time to enjoy the market at their leisure, and folks who might only have a few minutes before they have to get to work or another commitment. Since the LFM takes place on a weekday morning, it tends to have a particularly high proportion of shoppers in a hurry. You can do your part to support the market community by saving long chats with vendors for times without lines.

Safety first. This advice applies to the busy parking lot, as well. There's nothing you're in a hurry to get to that's more important than the safety of human beings, especially the little ones. Happily, we get lots of them at the market!

NOVEMBER

PAN-FRIED GARLIC PEA SHOOTS

SERVES 2

This easy recipe puts fresh winter veggies on the table in 5 minutes! It makes a nice addition to any winter main dish, or as a garnish for fish, pork chops, or chicken breast.

INGREDIENTS

2 tablespoons butter

1 bag pea shoots

3 cloves garlic, minced or pressed

1 tablespoon soy sauce

» Heat a sauté pan over medium-high heat. Add butter, sizzle, then add pea shoots and garlic. Cook, stirring, until slightly wilted, about 2 minutes.

» Add soy sauce, stir for another minute, and remove from heat. Serve immediately.

MIDDLEFIELD FARM

Located roughly halfway between Liverpool and Caledonia in Queens County, Middlefield Farm is a happy place for the Saunders family and their animals. Originally from Lancashire, England, Paul and Tracy Saunders had long dreamed of immigrating to Canada and a quieter pace of life. "There's no roosters now, so fairly quiet," Tracy jokes.

While they originally thought they might have a vegetable farm, the gift of some chickens from friends in Liverpool got them hooked on raising animals instead. Once they started to delve deeply into farming, Paul discovered he preferred working with the larger animals, while Tracy preferred looking after the birds.

Middlefield Farm has been coming to the Lunenburg Farmers' Market since December of 2021. They can also be found at the Chester Farmers' and Artisan Market on Fridays. Their meat and poultry offerings come from goats, chickens, turkeys, sheep, cattle, pigs, geese, and ducks. They keep egg chickens as well.

As someone who knows the animals best, Tracy also has some great advice for cooks: "Roast a chicken upside down to make the breast moister, and put some water in the pan—it makes a delicious gravy!" She likes to cut a whole lemon up

to put in the cavity of the bird and keeps a close eye on the thermometer, because birds raised on their style of farming cook through more quickly than most store-bought poultry.

"Our animals are grass-fed, free-range, and happy," says Tracy. "Just watching them when they're happy, and the great sense of satisfaction when someone says, 'That's the best turkey I've ever tasted,' keeps us going through the hard work."

INDONESIAN GOAT CURRY

SERVES 4

Paul Saunders from Middlefield Farm (see page 115) offers excellent options for goat meat for this recipe at the Lunenburg Farmers' Market.

INGREDIENTS

1 pound (454 grams) goat meat, cut into chunks

1 tablespoon minced fresh rosemary

one 2-inch piece fresh ginger, peeled and minced

1/2 teaspoon cumin

1 tablespoon coriander

1 teaspoon fennel seeds

1 tablespoon hot chili powder

1 teaspoon salt

1 teaspoon ground pepper

2 tablespoons extra-virgin olive oil, plus extra for pan

2 sweet potatoes, peeled and cut into bite-sized chunks

2 onions, diced

4 cloves garlic, minced or pressed

1 cup tomato sauce

2 cups water

1 tablespoon lemon juice

1/2 cup plain yogurt

» Preheat oven to 375°F (190°C). Lightly oil a large baking pan with olive oil and place the meat in the pan.

» In a small bowl, combine rosemary, ginger, cumin, coriander, fennel, chili powder, salt, pepper, and olive oil to make a marinade. Rub half of the marinade evenly over the meat.

» In a separate mixing bowl, combine sweet potatoes, onions, and garlic. Add the second half of the marinade and mix well. Add vegetable mixture, tomato sauce, water, and lemon juice to baking pan and toss well.

» Roast until all ingredients are tender, about 1 1/2 hours. Add yogurt, stir well, and serve.

ROSEMARY SCALLOPED POTATOES

SERVES 4

Potatoes, rosemary, and Havarti are a triumvirate of perfection. Break this recipe out when you want to impress somebody, including yourself. If you're preparing a holiday meal, this dish pairs well with the Garlic Honey Glazed Turkey recipe on page 132.

» Preheat the oven to 350°F (177°C) and butter a 9 x 12-inch baking dish.

» Arrange a layer of potato slices on the bottom of the baking dish, then cover them with a layer of Havarti and a sprinkle of rosemary. Alternate layers of potato and cheese, finishing with a layer of cheese on top.

» Gently drizzle cream over the cheese and potatoes, then season the top layer with remaining rosemary, salt, and pepper.

» Bake for 1 hour or until potatoes are browned on top and tender when stuck with a fork. Serve warm.

INGREDIENTS

3 large potatoes, cleaned, peeled, and cut into thin slices

3/4 cup thinly sliced or shredded Havarti cheese

1 tablespoon minced fresh rosemary

3/4 cup heavy cream

salt and pepper to taste

LEMON ROASTED SUNCHOKES

SERVES 4

Sunchokes (also called Jerusalem artichokes) are one of the many vegetables introduced to me by Wanda at Rumtopf Farm (page 83). They are an unparalleled delight, but make sure to limit yourself to a side dish portion at a time—where the "sun" goes, the wind will blow.

INGREDIENTS

1/2 pound (227 grams) sunchokes

1 tablespoon dried thyme

1/3 cup melted butter

1 tablespoon lemon juice

salt and pepper to taste

» Preheat oven to 375°F (190°C) and set aside a large baking pan.

» Clean sunchokes and either peel or leave unpeeled but cut out the eyes. Slice into coins.

» Mix all ingredients in the baking pan and toss until well combined. Spread out in an even layer. Roast until sunchokes are tender and starting to brown, 20–30 minutes.

PUMPKIN WHOOPIE PIES

SERVES 12

Pumpkin spice haters, move along. For the rest of you, this new take on an old-fashioned treat combines the best elements of cake, cookie, and festive flavours.

FOR THE COOKIES:

» Preheat oven to 350°F (177°C). Cover two baking sheets with parchment paper and set aside.

» With an electric beater, thoroughly beat butter and brown sugar together in a mixing bowl, then add pumpkin purée, eggs, and vanilla extract. Beat again.

» In a second bowl, whisk flour, baking soda, baking powder, cinnamon, ginger, and cloves together. Add dry ingredients to wet ingredients and mix until evenly combined.

» Using a soup spoon, drop spoonfuls of batter, spaced two inches apart, on prepared baking sheets. Bake until just baked through, 12–15 minutes. Transfer to wire racks and cool.

Continued on next page...

INGREDIENTS

For the cookies:

1 cup room temperature butter

2 cups packed brown sugar

2 cups pumpkin purée, either canned or homemade

2 large eggs

2 teaspoons vanilla extract

3 cups all-purpose flour

1 teaspoon baking soda

1 teaspoon baking powder

2 teaspoons ground cinnamon

2 teaspoons powdered ginger

1/2 teaspoon ground cloves

For the filling:

1 cup butter, room temperature

2 cups powdered sugar

one 213-gram jar marshmallow Fluff

1 tablespoon vanilla extract

FOR THE FILLING:

» Cream butter and powdered sugar together until fluffy, then add Fluff and vanilla. Beat until well combined.

» Fill whoopie pies by smoothing about 2 tablespoons of filling onto the flat side of one cookie, then top with another cookie, flat side also facing in.

» Assembled cookies can be stored, covered, in the refrigerator for several days. Bring to room temperature before serving.

DECEMBER

MaBell's

Seasonal Local MUSTARD

14th Century Lumbard Mustard

Ingredients: Ground Mustard
Wine Vinegar · Raisins · Sugar
Honey · Sea Salt

Seasonal Local JELLY

Savoury Curry & Red Onion

Ingredients: Red Onions · Raisins
Wine Vinegar · Sugar · Curry · Pectin

MaBell's

Seasonal Local JELLY

Garlicky Pepper Jelly

Ingredients: Garlic · Mixed Apples
Sugar · Wine Vinegar · Pectin

MaBell's

Seasonal Local CHUTNEY

Rhubarb Date & Apricot

Ingredients: Rhubarb · Dates · Sugar
Vinegar · Apricots · Onion · Ginger
Curry · Nutmeg

Seasonal Local JAM

Carrot & Cardamom

Ingredients: Carrots · Sugar · Lemons
Oranges · Cardamom · Pectin

SINCE FOREVER
MaBell's
COUNTRY CONDIMENTS

Seasonal Local JAM

Raspberry Jalapeño

Ingredients: Raspberries
Jalapeño · Lemon · Pectin

SINCE FOREVER
MaBell's
COUNTRY CONDIMENTS

Seasonal Local JAM

Drunken Strawberry

Ingredients: Strawberries · Sugar
Dry Sherry · Lemon Juice · Pectin

MaBell's

Seasonal Local JAM

Black Currant

Ingredients: Currants · Sugar

SINCE FOREVER
MaBell's
COUNTRY CONDIMENTS

Seasonal Local JAM

Raspberry & Vanilla

Ingredients: Raspberries · Sugar
Vanilla Bean

SINCE FOREVER
MaBell's
COUNTRY CONDIMENTS

MA BELL'S COUNTRY CONDIMENTS

Meredith Bell started her condiment business in 2006 and joined the LFM a few years later. Living rurally on four acres, she was able to forage ingredients and harvest berries, apples, and herbs from her land. "It started as a way to pay the bills," she says, "but I really got into it as a creative outlet. It was like being a bit of an alchemist." Meredith's offerings change through the seasons as she incorporates fresh ingredients into condiments. She's usually developing new flavours and she always has new ideas.

"I started to research a lot of the sort of history behind certain kinds of jams and jellies and what flavours seemed to work. And it also got me in touch with a lot of other local farmers or growers or people that had copious amount of berries that maybe I didn't grow enough [of] myself. It was a way to get to know people in the community and especially a lot of older people. So it became a community-based activity...a deep dive into the history of the area."

Meredith loves engaging with customers at the market, especially those who say they don't eat jam! "I say, 'Well, what brings you to the market?' If they're buying bread I might suggest a stuffed French toast. If people are meat-eaters then I would suggest a flavour that they could use for deglazing the pan to give them a sauce or a gravy that they hadn't thought about. I don't always have an answer, but often we come up with a solution together," she says, citing a customer who used her rosemary cracked peppercorn jelly on planked salmon as an example. "It would never have occurred to me to put rosemary with salmon, but now I can share that with other customers." And so she does, building community along the way.

BOSTOCK

SERVES 4

Traditional bostock is a luxurious alternative to French toast made with apricot jam, but we like to mix it up in our house. Use this recipe to explore any market jam that catches your fancy! I love it with Ma Bell's Raspberry and Vanilla Bean jam (see page 125). If you wish, you can use ground pecans or hazelnuts instead of almonds.

INGREDIENTS

1 loaf brioche (preferably slightly stale)

1 cup white sugar, divided

2 tablespoons lemon juice

1/3 cup water

2/3 cup ground almonds

6 tablespoons room temperature butter

1 large egg

2 tablespoons all-purpose flour

2 teaspoons vanilla extract

1/2 teaspoon salt

1/2 cup fruit jam

sliced almonds (optional)

icing sugar (optional)

» Preheat oven to 400°F (200°C). Line a rimmed baking sheet with parchment paper.

» Slice brioche into thick slices and place in a single layer on baking sheet. Set aside.

» Combine 1/2 cup of white sugar with the lemon juice and water in a small pot over medium-high heat. Cook, stirring, until sugar dissolves completely, about 5 minutes. Remove from heat and allow to cool slightly.

» While lemon syrup is cooling, mix remaining 1/2 cup of sugar, ground almonds, butter, egg, flour, vanilla extract, and salt in a large mixing bowl and beat until evenly combined. Set aside.

» Brush warm lemon syrup evenly over prepared brioche slices, then spread a thin layer of jam over each slice as well. Top with almond mixture.

» Bake until golden brown, about 15 minutes. Allow to cool slightly before serving. If desired, top with sliced almonds and icing sugar.

BRAISED BACON BRUSSELS SPROUTS

SERVES 4

Did you know that Brussels sprouts are a member of the cabbage family? If they aren't your thing, you can substitute another type of cabbage in this recipe.

» Cook the bacon and reserve the grease. Chop bacon into bite-sized pieces.

» Heat a sauté pan over medium heat. Add 2 tablespoons of bacon grease and sliced Brussels sprouts and sauté, stirring, for 5 minutes. Add chopped bacon, lemon juice, salt, and pepper and sauté for 1 minute more. Serve immediately.

INGREDIENTS

6 strips bacon

1 pound (454 grams) Brussels sprouts, cleaned and thinly sliced

1 teaspoon lemon juice

salt and pepper to taste

HASSELBACK SWEET POTATOES

SERVES 4

Hasselback potatoes are one of the fancier potato preparations out there, and very pretty on a holiday table. Luckily they aren't that difficult—just a lot of knife work. Make your slices as thin as you can manage without cutting all the way through.

INGREDIENTS

3 tablespoons melted butter

2 tablespoons maple syrup

1 tablespoon fresh thyme leaves

2 medium sweet potatoes, peeled and halved lengthwise

salt and pepper to taste

» Position a rack in the top third of the oven and preheat to 425°F (220°C). Oil a rimmed baking sheet and set aside.

» Combine melted butter, maple syrup, and thyme in a small mixing bowl and whisk well.

» Placing each sweet potato half with the cut half down, slice each one width-wise about 3/4 of the way through so that each potato half stays connected on the bottom. Make as many thin slices along the length of the potato as possible.

» Transfer sliced sweet potatoes to the prepared baking sheet, with the finely sliced edges facing up. Drizzle maple thyme butter evenly over the potatoes, then add salt and pepper to taste.

» Bake until tender and golden brown, about 30 minutes. Allow to cool slightly before serving.

GARLIC HONEY GLAZED TURKEY

SERVES 6–10

This is a tasty and attractive preparation for your holiday bird. If you prefer, you can add 1/4 cup of Sriracha to the glaze to spice it up!

INGREDIENTS

9–13 cloves garlic, divided

1/2 cup butter, melted

1/2 cup honey

1 tablespoon salt

1 turkey, any size, fresh or defrosted

» Peel then mince or press 5–8 cloves of garlic, as desired. Combine with melted butter, honey, and salt in a container and mix well. Set aside for 1 hour.

» Position a rack in the lower third of the oven and preheat to 315°F (160°C). Lightly butter a roasting pan large enough to hold your turkey. Place the turkey in the pan and place 4–5 peeled whole cloves of garlic in the body cavity.

» Pour the glaze over the turkey and brush over any uncovered surface.

» Roast, basting turkey with drippings from the bottom of the pan, until a meat thermometer in the thickest part of the thigh reads 165°F (75°C), 2–5 hours depending on the size of your turkey.

» Allow turkey to rest for 30 minutes before carving.

LAUGHING WHALE DESSERT COFFEE

SERVES 1

I depend on Laughing Whale coffee (page 14) to get me through the long days and nights of holiday baking, present wrapping, and cleaning—culminating in this cup to reward myself for successful completion!

» Combine coffee and sugar in a coffee mug and stir to dissolve sugar. Add rum, cinnamon stick, and zest (if using). Garnish with whipped cream if desired.

INGREDIENTS

1 cup Laughing Whale French roast coffee, brewed hot

2 teaspoons sugar

1/4 cup Ironworks rum

1 cinnamon stick

1 tablespoon Meyer lemon zest (optional)

whipped cream (optional)

MARKET TIP

LUNENBURG COUNTY LIGHTS

Whether you live in the Lunenburg area or are travelling through, there are a few other spots that a lover of the local and fresh just can't miss. Even though Boulangerie La Vendéenne sells at the market, their storefront in Blockhouse is well worth a visit for take-home pizza and ice cream. And while you're in Blockhouse, don't pass up farmer-and-more Camelia Frieberg's oasis, Chicory Blue General Store. A specialty foods store and restaurant, there's seating both upstairs and in the bucolic gardens adjacent to the Adventure Trail that connects Mahone Bay to Bridgewater.

If you're in Bridgewater, Fancy Pants Café is a must, as is Wile's Lake Farm Market just outside of town in Wileville. And in the town of Lunenburg itself, I can't talk about food without paying homage to Martin Ruiz Salvador's suite of restaurants: Beach Pea Kitchen & Bar, Salt Shaker Deli, Bar Salvador, The South Shore Fish Shack, and Half Shell Oyster Bar. Located within two blocks of each other in Lunenburg's bookstore district on Montague Street, all five establishments have menus inspired by the best local food the South Shore has to offer.

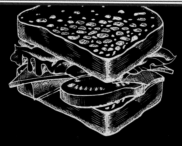

INDEX